Agile Project Management

The basics

Nate Jenner

Keywords: agile practical guide, agile methodology books, agile for beginners, agile process, agile book, agile for dummies, agile development, agile project management, agile handbook, agile programming, agile project management for dummies, management agile, what is agile, management artifacts, agile certification, define agile.

Table of Contents

Disclaimer

While all attempts have been made to verify the information provided in this book, the author does assume any responsibility for errors, omissions, or contrary interpretations of the subject matter contained within. The information provided in this book is for educational and entertainment purposes only. The reader is responsible for his or her own actions and the author does not accept any responsibilities for any liabilities or damages, real or perceived, resulting from the use of this information.

The trademarks that are used are without any consent, and the publication of the trademark is without permission or backing by the trademark owner. All trademarks and brands within this book are for clarifying purposes only and are the owned by the owners themselves, not affiliated with this document.

Introduction

Companies, individuals and organizations need proper and effective project management methodologies. For any project to be successful, it must be developed and delivered on time, within budget and meet the quality requirements expected by users. Most projects don't meet this. The reason is the user of ineffective project management methodologies. The traditional project management methodologies have been found to be ineffective and inapplicable to certain kinds of projects. Agile is a project management technique developed to solve problems associated with traditional project management techniques. Agile is popular for user involvement, regular delivery of working product and acceptance of changes even late in development. This book helps you familiarize yourself with agile project management techniques. Enjoy reading!

Chapter 1- Getting Started

Agile project management is one of the many methods used for project management. Initially, this project management method was solely used by IT professionals like software developers to manage their projects. However, the method has gained much acceptance in several other industries that are now using it to manage their diverse projects.

Software development has been in constant advancement, and the traditional methods have not been robust enough to cater for the needs. A good example of the traditional software development methods is waterfall. Nowadays, waterfall is not robust enough to cater for the requirements of software development, especially due to the fact that development of software products is done in a highly dynamic environment. The users keep on changing their requirements from time to time. The software development tools also change frequently. The traditional methods for software development could not handle these changing requirements.

There was a need for more flexible software development methods to handle the agility of requirements. This led to the development of agile project management method.

The information technology community was solely responsible for the development of this model, though it is now applicable in other types of industries.

Agile is a general term that is used to describe various methods that are used in agile development. A good example is *scrum*.

Chapter 2- The Agile Process

The agile development model differs with the traditional models in a number of ways.

First, in agile, there is an emphasis that the entire team should be a unit that is tightly integrated. This includes developers, customer, quality assurance and project management. This integration is made possible via frequent communication. Daily meetings are held to determine and discuss the work done during the day. Planning for the short-term events may also be done during the meeting.

Agile emphasizes on short-term deliveries. A delivery cycle normally ranges from one to four weeks. The cycles are normally referred to as *sprints*. The agile teams are allowed to express their views openly. This is achieved by use of open communication tools and techniques. The customers are also allowed to give their feedback quickly and openly. Any views and feedbacks obtained from the agile teams and the customers are considered when implementing the software. They serve as the basis for improvement and alignment to customer requirements. Due to early customer involvement in the project development process, agile teams have high chances of developing the right product.

This means that the end product will be accepted by users rather than being rejected. This is not the case with the traditional project development models like waterfall.

The Scope

In agile projects, the entire team takes the responsibility of managing the team rather than leaving it to the project manager. As far as procedures and processes are concerned, the team is allowed to follow common sense instead of written policies. This is a good way of ensuring that processes run faster and that there are no delays in decision making.

The agile project manager should possess leadership skills and motivate others in the agile team. This will help the team members retain the spirit and follow discipline as required. The project manager cannot be viewed as the boss to the agile team, but his work is to facilitate and coordinate all the resources and activities necessary for a speedy development.

Agile Project steps

The following are the necessary steps for one to complete an Agile project:

1. The product owner first identifies the product vision.

2. The product owner creates the product roadmap.

3. The product owner creates the release plan.

4. The product owner, the development team and the scrum master plan the sprints. The sprints are also known as iterations and products are created within the sprints.

5. During every sprint, the development team holds daily meetings commonly known as *scrums*.

6. The team holds the sprint review.

7. The team then holds the sprint retrospective.

User Stories

A user story refers to a requirement that defines what is needed by users as the functionality. The user story may be in any of the following two forms:

- As a <Role of User> I need <The Functionality> so that <The Business Value>

- In order to <The Business value> as a <Role of User> I need <The Functionality>

Note that in agile, the requirements for the product should be captured from the perspective of users. The user story should not be written on the perspective of the other stakeholders like testers, developers etc. During the release planning meeting, a relative scale is used as points to give a rough estimate to the user story. The story is further broken down into several tasks during the iteration planning. The product owner together with the team is responsible for writing the user stories. The product owner then takes the responsibility of explaining the user story to the development team. The product owner is also responsible for clarifying any questions raised by the development team about the user stories.

User stories are generated from functional characteristics. The product owner takes the responsibility of documenting the acceptance criteria. This should later be reviewed by the product owner together with the development team.

Relationship between User Stories and Tasks

1. A user story explains what is to be done. It is simply a definition of what the user needs.

2. Tasks explain how it will be done. It explains the steps or the methodology to be followed for implementation of the functionality.

3. The implementation of the stories is done by tasks. Every story is simply a collection of tasks.

4. When planning for a user story, it is divided into tasks. This is done when the user story is being planned for during the current iteration.

5. The estimation of tasks is done in hours, usually from 2 to 12 hours.

6. Validation of the user stories is done via acceptance tests.

Agile Artifacts

The progress of a project should be visible and measurable. The Agile teams use a number of artifacts to improve their effectiveness. The artifacts provide a strategic and tactic direction to the Agile team and radiate the progress of the project to the entire organization. The following are the artifacts used in Agile:

1. Product Vision Statement

This is a statement that states how the product supports the business objectives. The goals for the product are also states in this artifact. The product vision statement has high-level requirements for the product, and a loose time frame is stated on when those requirements will be implemented. It is responsible for defining the outermost boundary regarding what is covered in the project.

2. Product Roadmap
This artifact has high level requirements for the project, together with a loose timeframe of when those requirements are to be implemented.

3. Release Plan
The release plan states the timetable on how the working product will be released. It states the set of functionality from product roadmap that is viewed by the product owner as valuable for release into the marketplace. The release goal is responsible for stating the mid-term boundary around the specific functionality to be released to customers for use in real world.

4. Product Backlog
This artifact describes what is within the scope of the project, and it is ordered by priority. The product backlog is ready after getting your first requirement. It provides more details compared to the product

roadmap. Since the items of a product backlog are ordered, the items at the top have a higher priority compared to the ones at the bottom.

5. Sprint Backlog

This artifact has a list of items that are to be implemented in a particular sprint. These items are represented in the form of a sprint burn down chart, and kit serves to give the development team a way of checking whether they are on the right path towards meeting the goal of the sprint.

6. Increment

This is a fully functional and shippable product at the end of every sprint. I most cases, it adds functionality to what had been developed in the previous sprint.

Chapter 3- Agile Project Roles

The Agile teams have a high sense of urgency. The reason is that their core value is to respond to any changes that occur as far as the project is concerned. The Agile teams are aware of the dynamic nature of the software development environment. This is why adaptive planning is employed to exercise dynamic software development. Every role in the Agile team helps in forming a cohesive whole.

The members of the teams play different roles. The roles can be assigned different names depending on the methodology in use. Let us discuss the common roles in Agile:

Scrum Master

He acts as the coach to the development team. He or she is responsible for availing all the resources that the development team for the purpose of developing the product. He also guides the team on what to do and removes any barriers that may hinder them from doing their work. This helps to keep the team going. The work of the scrum master involves soft skills of project management rather than technical and planning skills. The latter are left to the team as a whole. Note that the scrum master is not the manager for the team.

The role reflects knowledge and responsibilities more than rank.

Product Owner

The product owner is responsible for representing the voice of the customers, increasing the return on investment (ROI) and is responsible for the prioritized product backlog. The product owner is responsible for documenting the requirements of the project and the user stories.

Team Members

The team members are responsible for the creation of a working product. The development team is normally composed of QA, developers and documentation. The development team members take the responsibility of planning, designing, developing, testing and delivering the project.

Stakeholders

This term represents a broad category of people including users, operations, managers of users, portfolio managers, support etc. They are the people who have an interest in the project, or the ones who will be affected by the project in one way or another.

Other than the roles discussed above, the Agile teams sometimes consider to call other people who provide technical or domain expertise when necessary. These are the people who possess some professional skills that the Agile team members may not possess. Also, it is not reasonable for the product owners to be experts and each domain. This is why they sometimes have to call for expertise from external sources.

Chapter 4- Agile Events

During Agile development, there are a number of events that are held. It is during these events that the development team gets time to evaluate, organize and make necessary adjustments. Let us discuss the common events in Agile project management:

Sprint Planning Meeting

This is a meeting held at the start of each sprint. It is during this meeting that the scrum team plans for the sprint and identifies its scope, goals and the sprint backlog items to be implemented during the sprint. In short, the development team just discusses what they will be doing during the sprint. The kind of increment to be delivered at the end of the sprint may also be defined.

Daily Scrum Meeting

This type of event is held on a daily basis for not more than 15 minutes. The following three statements are made during the daily scrum meeting:

1. What every team member accomplished yesterday.

2. What every team member will work on today.

3. The list of items that is impending the team member.

Sprint Review Meeting

The sprint review is a meeting held at the end of every sprint, during which the development team demonstrates a working product to the stakeholders and entire organization. This is normally the product that was developed during the sprint.

Sprint Retrospective

The sprint retrospective is also held at the end of each sprint, during which the team discusses what went well, what could be changed and how the changes can be made. The team involves the product owner, the scrum master and the development team members. The improvements that can be made in the next sprint are also identified and discussed. At the end of the meeting, the team comes with tangible improvement plans for the next sprint.

Chapter 5- Agile Manifesto

Agile follows a manifesto that should be followed so as to ensure that the end product is of the quality expected by the users. The following are the twelve principles of the agile manifesto:

1. Customer satisfaction
There is an early and continuous delivery of a working product to the customers, which is a good way of satisfying customers.

2. Welcome change
Software development is done in a very dynamic environment, hence changes are inevitable. Agile allows for changes even in the late stages of development. The agile process usually works while increasing the user's competitive advantage.

3. Deliver working software
Working software should be delivered frequently. The delivery period should be within a short range of few weeks to few months. The delivery is done based on what was agreed with the other stakeholders.

4. Collaboration
The developers and the business people must work together during the entire development process. This way, the development team will stay on the right

track and the end-product will be acceptable to the users.

5. Motivation

The individuals taking part in the project development should be motivated. An environment that supports the team members should be created. The members should also be trusted so that they may take up the responsibility of getting the job done.

6. Face-to-Face communication

For the development work to run smoothly, communication should be done effectively for correct messages to be relayed to development team. Face-to-face communication is used as the method of communication and relaying information to the development team.

7. Progress is Measured based on Working Software

The key is agile project management is delivery of a working software, and this is used as the measure of progress. The progress is analyzed by determining the amount of functionality that has been implemented so far.

8. Maintain constant pace

The goal of agile processes is achieving a sustainable development. The developers, the business and the users should be capable of maintaining a constant pace with the project under development.

9. Monitoring
Regular attention should be paid to good design and technical excellence to enhance agility.

10. Simplicity
Everything should be kept simple and simple terms should be used to measure the work that is yet to be done.

11. Self-Organized Teams
Agile teams are expected to be self-organized but not to heavily depend other teams. This is the key to best requirements, architectures and designs. Review the Work Regularly.

The work done should be reviewed on a regular basis for the team to reflect on how to become more effective then take the necessary measures to adjust their behavior accordingly.

Chapter 6- Daily Stand-up

A daily standup is a meeting held daily by the agile team to report on their progress. Other than providing the agile team members to report on their progress, it provides them with an opportunity to present their problems to be tackled. This meeting must be held daily regardless of how the agile team has been setup or the geographical location of its members. The meeting is usually held for about 15 minutes.

Every member of the agile team is expected to answer questions about the following:

- What they did the previous day.

- What they will do today.

- Any impendent that they may be facing.

The daily stand-up is held to report on the status of the project, but it's not a discussion meeting. If there is a need for discussion, the team members are expected to hold another meeting at a different time. To ensure the meeting ends quickly, the members should stand rather than sit.

Benefits of the Daily Stand-Up

The following are the benefits of holding a daily stand-up:

1. The team can assess the progress and determine whether they can deliver according to the iteration plan.

2. Each team member will state their commitments during the day. This way, they can predict what they can achieve at the end of the day.

3. The team can spot any delays or obstacles as they work on the project.

The Attendants

The stand-up should be attended by the product owner, the scrum master and the delivery team. The customers and the stakeholders are encouraged to attend the meeting, during which they can simply act as observers. However, these are not allowed to take part in the daily stand-ups. The scrum master takes the responsibility of noting any queries from the team members as well as the problems they may be facing.

What if the Teams are Geographically Dispersed?

There are different ways to conduct a daily stand-up, making it possible to hold it even when the teams are operating from different office locations. Different locations mean different time zones. Each team, that is, those operating from the same office can hold their stand-up at their own and update their status on a tool like SharePoint, Rally, Wikis etc.

For communication, the team should use video conferencing, conferencing call, instant messengers and others. These will facilitate sharing of knowledge amongst the teams.

Chapter 7- Definition of "Done"

The team is responsible for defining the meaning of the word "done". The following criteria may be used:

1. All the tasks have been completed.

2. All the acceptance tests are running.

3. There is no open defect.

4. The story has been accepted by the product owner.

5. A deliverable has been made to the end-user.

The acceptance criteria simply refer to the behavior, functionality and performance that are required by a feature to be accepted by product owner. It simply defines what is to be done for the developer to know when a user story is complete.

User Story

Requirements are usually transformed into user stories in the language of the user. The user story must be implemented in the current iteration. A user is said to be done when:

- All the related code has been checked-in.

- All unit test cases have already been passed.

- All acceptance test cases have already been passed.

- Help text has been written.

- The story has been accepted by the Product Owner.

Iteration

Iteration refers to a time-boxed collection of several user stories or defects that are to be worked upon and accepted during the product release. The iterations are normally planned during iteration planning meeting then completed with a review meeting or iteration demo. Iteration can also be referred to as a *sprint*. Iteration may be done under any of the following conditions:

- When the product backup is completed.

- After testing of product performance.

- User stories have been moved to next iteration or they have been accepted.

- Defects have been postponed to next iteration or they have been fixed.

Release

This is a milestone marked by the delivery of a working product. The product can be internal or external, and it must first be tested before being released. A release is said to be done after:

- The system has been stress tested.

- The performance has been tuned.

- Security validations have been carried out.

- A disaster recovery plan has been tested.

Chapter 8- Release Planning

The goal of release planning is to come up with a plan to help deliver an increment to the product under development. This is done after 2 to 3 months.

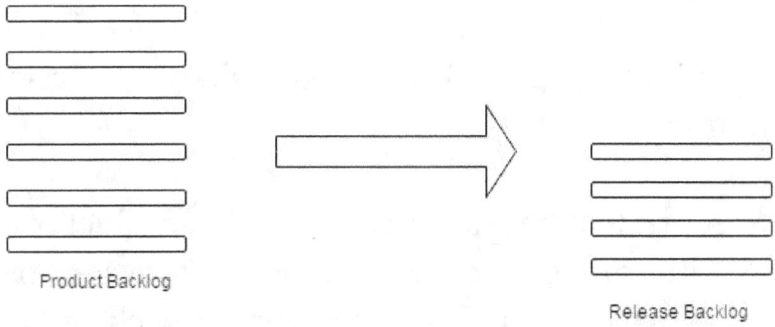

Product Backlog

Release Backlog

The Participants

The following agile members take part in the release planning:

1. Scrum Master- the scrum master is the facilitator of the agile delivery team.

2. Product Owner- He or she represents the general view of product backlog.

3. Agile Team- the Agile Delivery Team is responsible for providing on technical feasibilities or any existing dependencies.

4. Stakeholders- these include program managers, customers and subject matter experts who act as the advisors when decisions are being made during the release plan meeting.

Prerequisites

The following are the prerequisites for release planning:

1. A product backlog created by the product owner with ranked items. The product owner picks about 10 items from the product backlog based on what he thinks should be implemented in the release.

2. The input of the team about capabilities, the known velocity and any technical challenge.

3. A high-level vision.

4. Market and the Business objective.

5. An acknowledgement on whether there is a need for the new product backlog items.

Required Materials

The following are the materials needed for the release planning:

- Posted purpose, agenda.

- Whiteboards, flip charts and markers. These will be used for any presentations and making writings if necessary.

- A project and a way to connect computers for data sharing during the meeting.

- The planning data.

Planning Data

For a plan to be created during the release planning, some data is required. This includes the following:

- The previous iterations or results from previous iterations.

- Feedback from the previous stakeholders regarding the market conditions, product and deadlines.

- Action plans for the previous iterations/releases.

- The defects or features that are to be considered.

- The velocity from the previous estimates or releases.

- Personal and organizational calendars.

- Inputs from the other teams for controlling any dependencies.

Release Planning Output

The following are the outputs obtained from the release planning:

- Commitment.

- Release plan.

- Concerns, issues, assumptions ad dependencies that need to be monitored.

- Suggestions that are needed to improve on the future release planning.

The Agenda

The agenda for a release plan may be as follows:

- Opening Ceremony- this includes a welcome message, agenda and purpose review, organizing the necessary tools and an introduction to the business sponsors.

- Product Roadmap/ Vision- this describes a large picture of the project.

- A review of previous releases- this involves a discussion about any item that may have an impact on the plan.

- Release name/theme- this involves an inspection of the current status of the roadmap themes and perform any adjustments that may be needed.

- Velocity- this involves a presentation of the velocity of the current release and previous releases.

- Release schedule- this is a review of the key milestones and decision on boxes for the iterations within the release.

- Issues and concerns- you should check for any issues or concerns the record them.

- Review then Update Definition of "Done"- the definition of the word "done" should be reviewed regularly and any necessary changes made based on skill, technology or any changes made to the team members since the last release/iteration.

- Stories and items for consideration- The features and user stories from the product backlog that should be considered in the current release should be presented. This will help the development team members know what they will be working on during the iteration.

- Determining sizing values- in case the velocity is not known, you should plan for the sizing values to be used during the release planning.

- Sizing the stories- the agile delivery team should consider the correct size of the user stories under consideration then divide the stories into iterations in case the story is too large. The subject matter expert and the product owner clarify expound the doubts, determine the acceptance criteria then carry out the splitting. The scrum master should take the responsibility of facilitating the collaboration.

- Map the stories to iterations- The product owner and the delivery team move the defects/stories in the iterations depending on the velocity and size. The scrum master should take the responsibility of facilitating the collaboration.

- New issues or concerns- new issues and concerns from the previous experience should be checked and recorded.

- Assumptions and Dependencies- any assumptions or dependencies planned during the release planning should be checked.

- Commit- the scrum master should notify the agile members about the planning. If the product owner and the development team reach an agreement as the best plan, they commit to go ahead to the next step of planning, that is, iteration planning.

- Communication and logistics planning- the logistics and communications planning for the release should be reviewed and updated.

- Parking lot- In this step, all the product backlog items should be resolves or be set as action plans.

- Distribute action plans and actions items- the action items should be distributed amongst the owners, then the action plan should be processed.

- Retrospect- this involves getting feedback from the participants to ensure the meeting was successful.

- Close- in this step, success is celebrated.

Chapter 9- Iteration Planning

During the iteration planning, the agile team meets to identify the top-ranked items in the product backlog that they can commit to complete during the coming iteration. The work is summarized as committed iteration goals. This commitment is usually time boxed depending on the length of the iteration and the velocity of the team.

The teams begin by choosing some items from the product backlog then commits to complete them during the incoming iteration. The backlog of the team has been seeded and planed partially. Also, the team already has feedback from the earlier iterations as well as from other teams and system demo.

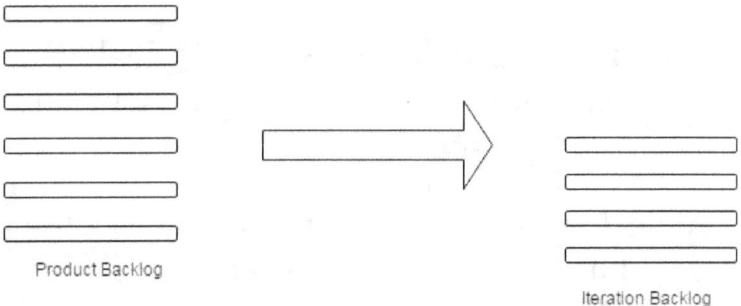

Product Backlog

Iteration Backlog

The iteration planning helps in organizing the work and defining a realistic scope for the iteration. Each Agile team agrees on the set of stories for upcoming iteration then summarizes them into iteration goals.

The iteration goals and backlog are determined by the capacity of the team and allows for the analysis of the complexity, dependencies and size of each story on other teams and other stories. By the end of the meeting, the teams should have committed to the goals of the iteration and adjusted the stories to get to the larger purpose. The management will not change the scope of the iteration, and the team can focus on its goals.

The Participants

The following agile members take part in iteration planning:

1. Scrum Master- the scrum master takes the responsibility of facilitating the agile team.

2. Product Owner- he or she will deal with the product backlog in a detailed view and the acceptance criteria.

3. Agile Team- the team defines the tasks they will do during the iteration and estimates the amount of effort that is needed to fulfill the commitment.

Prerequisites

The following are the prerequisites to the iteration planning:

- The product backlog items should be sized and a relative story point assigned to them.

- The product items should have been ranked by the product owner.

- The acceptance criteria for every portfolio item should have been defined.

The Agenda

An iteration planning should follow the steps given below:

- Identify the number of stories that can fit in the iteration.

- Break the stories into tasks then assign every task to its owner.

- Each task is given a time estimate in hours.

- The estimates will help the team members to check the number of task hours every member has for the iteration.

- The tasks are assigned to team members based on their capacity or velocity to avoid overburdening them.

Here is an example agenda for the iteration planning:

1. Calculate the capacity of the team for the iteration.

2. Discuss every story, elaborate the acceptance criteria then provide estimates via story points.

3. The planning will only stop once the team has run out of capacity.

4. Determine then reach an agreement about the iteration goals.

5. Everyone should now commit to the goals.

The acceptance criteria should be established via a conversation and collaboration with product Owner while featuring other stakeholders. The Product Owner may decide to change how the stories are ranked depending on story estimates. The team may also choose to divide the stories to get tasks and the approximate hours. The team will then collectively execute the tasks.

For an iteration meeting to run successful, follow these guidelines:

- The meeting should be time boxed for 4 hours or less.

- The planning session should be organized by the team and it is for the team.

- The team should not commit to the work that exceeding its historical velocity.

Calculating the Velocity

The agile team relies on past relies to estimate the velocity. Velocity refers to the average number of iterations that are required to finish the user stories in iteration. For example, if the team had taken 10, 12 and 14 story points in the last three iterations, then it can use 12 story points in the next iteration. The planned velocity will tell the team the number of stories that they can complete in current iteration. If the assigned tasks are completed quickly, more user stories may be pulled in. It is also possible to pull out stories to next iteration.

Task Capacity

The following facts are used to get the capacity of a team:

- The number of real hours worked in a day.

- The number of days available for the person in the iteration.

- The percentage of time that a member is available for team.

Suppose we have a team of 10 members ready to work full time on the project, that is, 8 hours in a day. Also, no team member will leave the as the iteration goes on. If the iteration runs for 1 week, then the task capacity can eb calculated as follows:

10 × 8 × 1 = 80 hours

During the iteration planning, the product owner must first describe the items with the highest ranking in the product backlog. The team then describes all tasks needed to complete the item. The team members will own the tasks. The team members perform an estimate to determine the time required for completion of each task. The same steps must be followed to complete all items for the iteration. For the case of individuals who are overloaded with tasks, their tasks should be distributed to the other members.

Chapter 10- The Role of Product Backlog

The product backlog is the artifact with the list of items that are to be done. The product backlog items are ranked according to feature descriptions. In most cases, the items are broken down and organized in the form of user stories.

The following are the reasons why the product backlog is important:

1. It helps in giving estimates to every feature of the product.

2. It helps the agile team plan a roadmap for the project.

3. It is good for re-ranking the product features for an improved value of the product.

4. It is good for knowing what should be prioritized first. The team will rank the items then build value.

Features of a Good Product Backlog

A good product backlog should have the following features:

1. Each product should have a single product backlog with features organized from the large to the largest features.

2. It is possible for multiple teams to work on the product backlog.

3. The ranking of the product backlog features should be done based on technical value, business value, strategic or risk management fitness.

4. The highest-ranking items are factored into smaller stories to give them during the release planning. These will be worked on in the future iterations.

Chapter 11- Retrospective Meeting

At the sprint's end, the team holds a retrospective meeting. During the meeting, they discuss what happened during the sprint, identifying what was run well and what happened wrongly. Any action items that should be carried over to the next sprint are also identified during the meeting. The retrospective meetings are a good way for making a continuous improvement in an Agile team.

Some of the topics for discussion during the retrospective meeting include metrics, the tracking tools, and the velocity of the team, team dynamics, defect density, self-organization and the impediments that were faced during the iteration. With the retrospectives, we may end up with coverage improvements, giving more importance to test strategy, unit testing and test plans. The root causes for the various issues related to testing may be identified and any necessary actions suggested. This means that it helps the team perform continuous testing and improvement.

For every iteration, it is possible to hold each retrospective at the same location. The testers will then bring in their unique testing perspective and experience to the retrospective.

The Product Owner, the Scrum Master and the team are all encouraged to attend the retrospective.

Senior management such as the managers may not be allowed to attend the retrospective. The reason is that the agile team members may fear to talk due to the fear of authorities. The retrospective has an ecosystem of openness and mutual trust.

The retrospective can be run by simply asking the participants different questions. It's not a must for you to ask about what went well or what didn't go well. You can ask the following:

1. What should we begin to do?

2. What should we avoid doing?

3. What should we keep on doing?

The teams are encouraged to give specific answers so that the right action may be taken. The retrospective meeting should be held immediately after sprint review meeting. The entire team is also encouraged to participate. This way, all issues or concerns faced during previous sprint will be addressed and avoided in the coming sprints.

Chapter 12- Continuous Integration

Continuous integration refers to a process in which all the local working code base for the developer is merged to share with common repository severally during product development.

Continuous integration was first adopted in extreme programming (XP). Continuous integration helps developers avoid stepping on the code from the other developers and eliminates issues to do with integration. Continuous integration goes hand-in-hand with configuration management, software build, compilation, deployment and testing. These are all combined into a single, automated and repeated process.

Since the code is integrated rapidly, there are high chances that the defects will surface quickly compared to manual integration. The following is the built-in automation for continuous integration that helps it check for the validity of the checked in code:

1. Statistical code analysis- this helps in reporting the results obtained from statistical code analysis.

2. Compile- this involves the generation of executable files by linking code then compiling after.

3. Unit test- this involves writing unit tests, running them, checking code average then reporting the results.

4. Deploy- the code is build then deployed or installed in a working/production environment.

5. Integration test- performing integration tests to provide results.

6. Report (dashboard)- the status of the key parameters is shown by posting Green, Red and Yellow in a location that is visible to the public.

With continuous integration, testers can perform automation more effectively and identify any defects faster than improve on the regression results. Testers will also be relieved from the task of performing manual tests. This helps in reducing the amount of time taken to deliver a working product. It is also easy to maintain different versions of the product with much ease.

Chapter 13 - Agile Quality Tools

There are many and different types of agile tools. Some can be obtained for free while others are on sale. There are also numerous enterprise tools supporting end-to-end flow of software development life cycle such as requirements management, defect tracking and test management. Let us discuss some of the tools that can be used for quality improvement in agile project management:

Flow Chart

This tool helps the developers and other stakeholders analyze the flow of project events. It helps in mapping events that flow either sequentially or in parallel. In case of complex events, a flow chart can help the agile teams to analyze them and find any interdependencies between the events. One can also determine the critical path for the processes and the events that are taking place in the critical path. The critical path is the set of events that must not be delayed at all; otherwise, the entire project will be delayed.

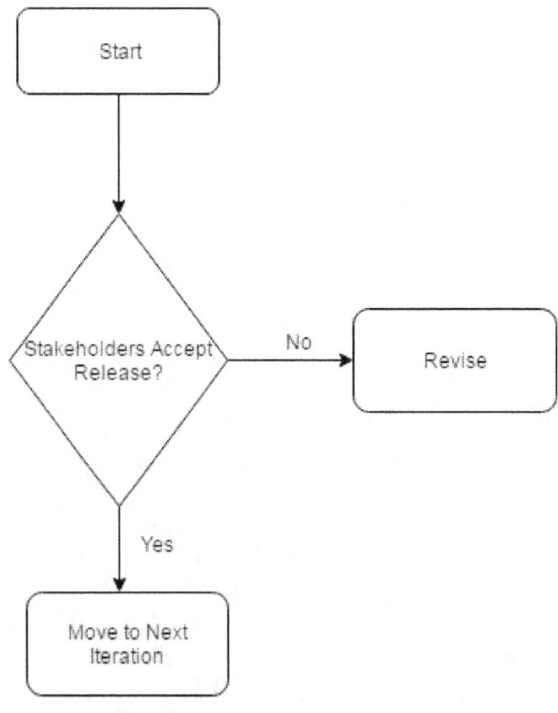

Burndown Chart

This tool can be used in agile to track the total work that is remaining and determine the likelihood of achieving the sprint goal. This will help the team track and manage their progress and respond accordingly. With a burndown chart, one can graphically show the trend of remaining to do tasks for the sprint. Here is an example of a sprint burndown chart:

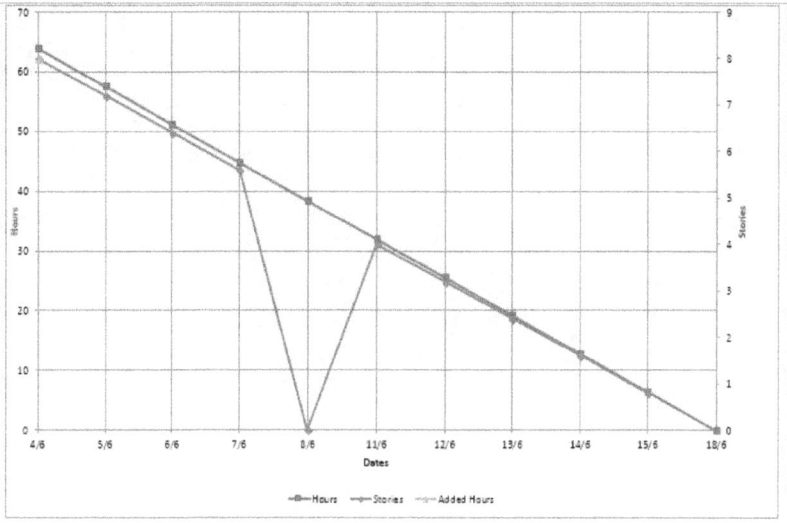

When creating a plan or working on an iteration, the team should track their progress in terms of where they have reached in relation to the whole release plan. When the teams are busy to ensure that the iterations are delivered successfully, they forget about their progress against release goals.

An additional scope may be added as the team's works hard to march forward. Due to this, the team may forget to report their progress to the organization. The burndown chart may help prevent this.

Velocity Chart

This is a good tool for tracking the amount of work that is completed from sprint to sprint. It helps one estimate the velocity of a team and performs an estimate of the amount of work that a team can complete in the future sprints. In agile, velocity is used as a way of measuring the rate at which scrum teams consistently deliver the business value. The velocity of an agile team can be calculated by adding the estimates of features, requirements, user stories or backlog items that have been completed successfully during iteration.

Before you can complete the first iteration, it may be a bit tricky for you to estimate the velocity of your team. However, several ways are provided through which you can do it. After that, you can use history to estimate the velocity of your team for each iteration. This way, you will have a consistent way of making improvements to the agile processes and the teams.

It is easy for you to draw a velocity chart. It is simply a graph showing the iterations on the X-axis and the number of points on the Y-axis. The points represent the velocity of the team for the various iterations. An example is shown below:

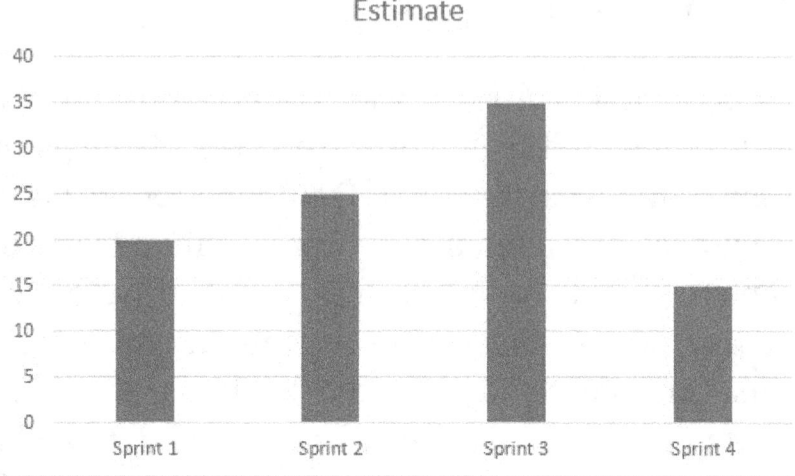

Estimate

We have 4 sprints for the project, but the velocity of the team is different for each sprint.

Pareto Charts

This is a good tool for identifying the set of priorities that you have. In agile, it can be used to analyze the items contained in product backlog. After the analysis, the agile team will be able to tell the product backlog items that should be given the highest priority during the prioritization of the items. This way, the stakeholders will be satisfied with the way increments are delivered.

With agile, customer feedback is necessary. When properly analyzed, the team will make the necessary improvements. A Pareto chart can help the agile team analyze complaints from the users about the product and take the necessary action to remedy and avoid this in the future sprints. An example of a Pareto chart is given below:

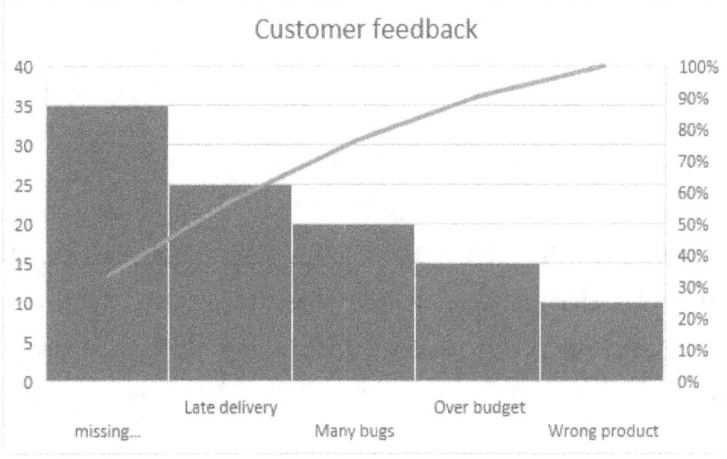

Epic Report

This report helps the team understand the progress they have made towards the completion of an epic overtime. The tool helps in the management of the progress of the team by tracking the amount of incomplete work that is remaining.

An epic refers to a functionality or feature that is completed within a span of sprints. An epic report clearly shows the complete, incomplete and the un-estimated issues in an epic. It is a good tool for estimating the work of an epic that may be extending for several sprints. It will help you understand the progress that you have made towards completing the epic overtime, and track the amount of work that is incomplete or un-estimated.

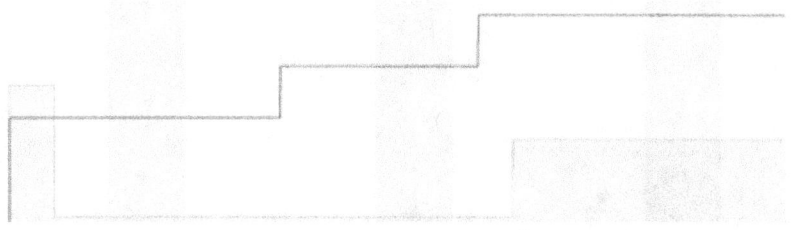

The epic report will show you the amount of effort required to do work for the epic in every sprint. The issues faced in each sprint to create the epic will also be shown.

Control Chart

This is a good tool for showing you the cycle time for the version, product or sprint. This way, one can tell whether the data obtained from the current process may be used to determine future performance. The tool will help you manage the progress of the entire agile process. With a control chart, you can tell how stable the agile process is about developing your product. You can also make a prediction about the outcome of the process or any sprint. A control chart is a good way of identifying the common cause variation. The control chart has limits that represent the expected limits of variation both below and above the data average. The limits are calculated mathematically and indicated using dotted lines. Here is an example of a control chart:

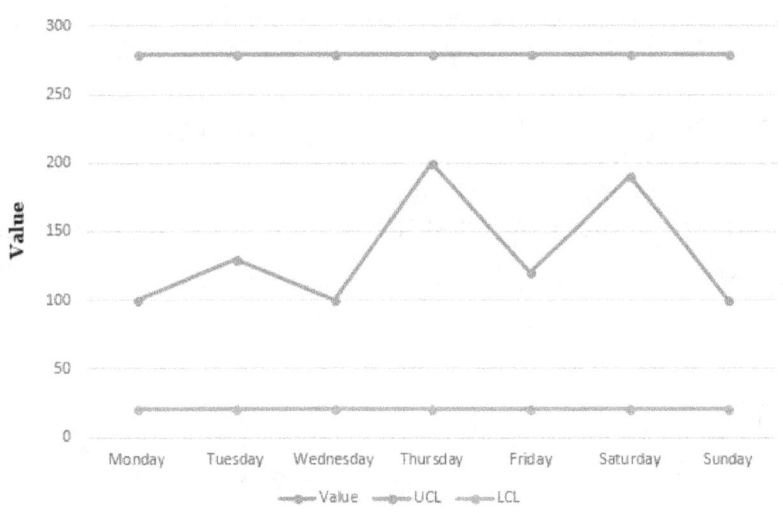

Chapter 14- Effort Estimation

In sprint zero, the agile team already has the effort estimation for all stories in the release. Planning poker is an exercise for effort estimation and it makes sure that every member of the team takes part in the effort estimation exercise.

The planning poker technique works based on a consensus and it can be used for effort estimation or sizing of the stories. It's a non-linear scale of estimation technique. The planning poker relies on Fibonacci numbers with the higher numbers rounded off. If for example you are asked to give an estimate of a user story, your estimate will be rounded to one of the numbers contained in the Fibonacci series.

Suppose the Fibonacci series under use has the following numbers:

0, 0.5, 1, 2, 3, 4, 8, 14, 20, 45, 60, 110

If you are asked to estimate the duration for a task you state its 10 days, then your answer will be rounded off to either 8 or 14.

Each member of the team takes a deck of cards then estimates each story without being interfered with.

The following steps are used for estimation in the planning poker technique:

1. The product owner describes a user story and its acceptance criteria to the team in detail.

2. The team discusses the work to be done for the user story and the team members ask any questions they may have.

3. Every member makes an estimate for the story without the influence of others.

4. Every member selects a poker card that reflects the estimate they have given to the effort required for the user story.

5. All members reveal their estimates at once.

6. The members who had chosen lowest and highest estimates are given a chance to explain their reason behind the estimate. Neutralization of any misunderstandings is done.

7. Once the discussion is over, the members reselect the cards for their new estimates based on the discussion.

8. The final number agreed by the members is taken as the estimate.

9. The same steps are repeated for all the stories in the product backlog.

Planning poker makes estimation of effort fun. The technique ensures that every member takes part and is on same page with other members in understanding the requirements of each user story in the product backlog.

Chapter 15- Testing in Agile

The agile testing techniques are closely related to their traditional counterparts. However, variations may be needed in agile because of variances brought about by techniques, documentation and jargon.

The requirements for the agile projects outflow in the form of user stories with the product owner and the team taking the responsibility of writing the user stories. The user stories should follow a prescribed format right from the point of end user. The user stories are kept in the product backlog in a prioritized manner. The user stories also have the acceptance criteria with the story requirements being explained in brief. Some of the components of the acceptance criteria may include non-functional requirements, the scope conditions and quality conditions. It is good to relate the user stories to testable outcome, and they will pave way for agile architectures that are incremental. Here are examples:

- Previous learning and expert judgment.

- Current features, technical features and architecture functionality.

- User personas (including system configurations, and user behavior).

- The tools and quality of deployed code.

- Wireframes that act as mockups.

- Defect density from the current and the previous iterations.

- Any applicable regulatory standards, example, IEEE, SOX, FDA.

- Risks and the system quality.

The task of the development team is to implement the user stories in every iteration, with strings attached such as code checked in, verifiable quality built in and code validated via acceptance testing.

Conclusion

This marks the end of this book. Agile is a project management methodology with a great emphasis on user involvement. With agile, changes to the product can be accepted even in the late stages of the development process. This isn't the case with traditional development methodologies like waterfall. Agile teams continuously involve users. The users provide feedback regarding the progress of the project and the quality of the product that has been developed so far. This helps the agile development team make changes and improvements that may be necessary. Due to the continuous user involvement in the development process, there are high chances of developing the right product. This also means there are high chances of developing an acceptable product.

Note that Agile is used to represent a set of project development methodologies like scrum, Kanban etc. Agile was initially developed to be used for development of software products. However, agile has been adopted successfully in other industries for project development. This means that agile is applicable in various fields. It was developed to help improve and solve the problems experienced by project developers who used traditional project development methodologies.

www.ingramcontent.com/pod-product-compliance
Lightning Source LLC
Chambersburg PA
CBHW071236220526
45468CB00002B/885